Lettering

in
CRAZY
Cool
Quirky
Style

by the editors
of Klutz

KLUTZ®

KLUTZ® is a kids' company staffed entirely by real human beings. We began our corporate life in 1977 in an office we shared with a Chevrolet Impala. Today we've outgrown our founding garage but Palo Alto, California, remains Klutz galactic headquarters. For those of you who collect corporate mission statements, here's ours:

Create Wonderful Things
Be Good   Have Fun

Distributed in the UK by
Scholastic UK Ltd
Westfield Road
Southam, Warwickshire
CV47 0RA England

Distributed in Australia by
Scholastic Australia Customer Service
PO Box 579
Gosford NSW 2250
Australia

Book printed in China.
All other parts manufactured in China.

KLUTZ®
450 Lambert Avenue
Palo Alto, CA 94306

Write Us
We would love to hear your comments regarding this or any of our books. We have many!

Visit Our Website
You can check out all the stuff we make, find a nearby retailer, sign up for a newsletter, e-mail us or just goof off.

ISBN 1-57054-428-X
4 1 5 8 5 7 0 8 8 8

KLUTZ.com
Come on in!

It's easy to put your feelings into words. To really get your point across, though, try putting your feelings into LETTERS.

This book comes with everything you need to make letters that are just as expressive as words. Use them carefully. Anything you write in letters like this will have real

ALL THESE SUPPLIES COME WITH THIS BOOK.

Making Cool letters takes focus. We've found it works best to... work on a flat, well-lit surface ☼ listen to your favorite music ♪ keep pesky siblings out of the room.

8 double-pointed
COLORED PENCILS
Keep your pencil point sharp but short. Really long pencil points tend to break.

pencil
SHARPENER
For crisp color and fine lines, sharpen the colored pencils frequently.

50 sheets of
PRACTICE PAPER

5 plastic
STENCILS

2 sheets of
STICKER PAPER

☺ Design your own sticker artwork on the front side.

☺ Peel off the back to expose the stickiness.

4 felt-tip
MARKERS

Keep the markers capped when you're not using them so they don't dry out.

Push to make lead come out.

a white
ERASER

MECHANICAL PENCIL

☺ Click out only a little lead at a time, so the tip is not too long.

☺ Keep your pencil marks light. Writing lightly keeps the lead from breaking and makes your pencil marks easier to erase.

Use this stuff, along with your own favorite art supplies, to make letters that spell out your own Cool Style.

5

SIMPLE STENCILS

The easiest way to make perfectly perfect letters is to use stencils. Here's how:

1 Use the ruler edge of the blue stencil to lightly pencil a baseline across your page.

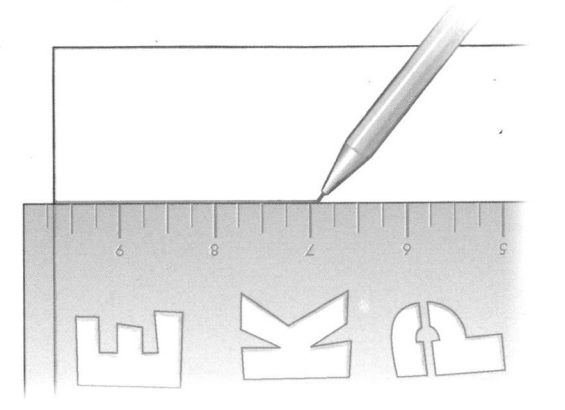

2 Lay the stencil on your paper so the letter you want to make is sitting right on the baseline.

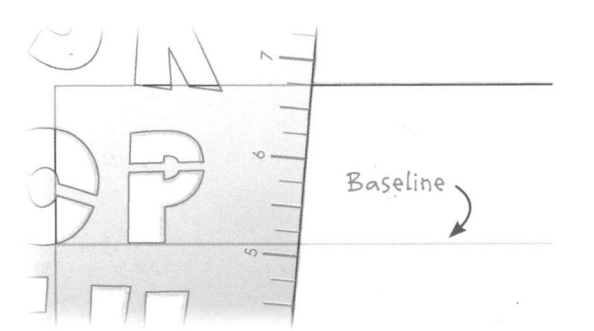

Baseline

3 Run your pencil all the way around inside the letter shape, pressing against the edge of the stencil as you go.

Keep your pencil marks light on the paper.

If the letter you are stenciling has an extra horizontal bar running through it, just hop your pencil over the bar and keep outlining.

Ta-da!
You've made your first letter!

4 Line up your second letter next to the first. Move the stencil around until the spacing looks right to you.

Pay attention to the space you leave between the letters: They shouldn't touch each other, but there shouldn't be a huge gap between them, either.

5 Run your pencil around the second letter stencil. Keep adding letters this way until you've finished the word.

6 Use your pencil to smooth out any hiccups in the letters and fill in any gaps left by the stencils (unless you like the gaps).

Keep your pencil marks light!

If you perch a rounded letter, like an O, on the baseline like all the other letters, it might look weirdly tall and goofy. Let the bottom of the O hang a little bit below the baseline and it looks O.K.

7 Outline your letters in marker pen. Once the pen has dried completely (this usually takes just a few seconds), erase the pencil marks, including the baseline.

8 Color in the letters any way you like.

CHUNKY
STENCIL LETTERS

Make fat stencil letters look even heftier with this 3-D effect.

1 Use the ruler edge of the blue stencil to pencil a straight baseline. Then slide the stencil down a tiny bit and pencil in another baseline right below the first one.

The space between the two baselines should be really tiny, about 1/16" (1.5mm).

2 Use the mechanical pencil to stencil your first letter so it's perched on the lower baseline. Go over the pencil with marker pen.

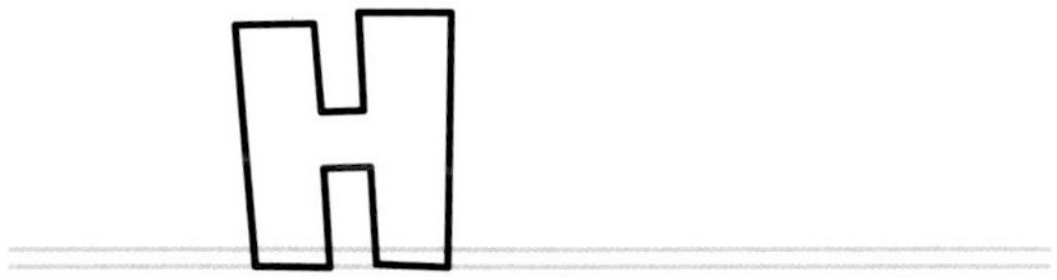

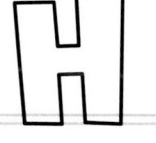

3 Perch the same letter stencil on the upper baseline so it's a little off-center from the first letter. The two letters should overlap each other almost completely. Pencil the stencil as usual.

4 Now you have two overlapping letters. Imagine that together they make one solid object: The pen letter is the front of the object and the pencil letter is the back.

Use your mechanical pencil to make little diagonal lines connecting the corners of the pen letter with the corners of the pencil letter.

5 With a marker, go over just those pencil lines that you want to keep.

If this H were solid you wouldn't see these lines, so don't ink them.

6 After the ink has dried, erase the pencil lines. Add more letters the same way and decorate your chunky word any way you want.

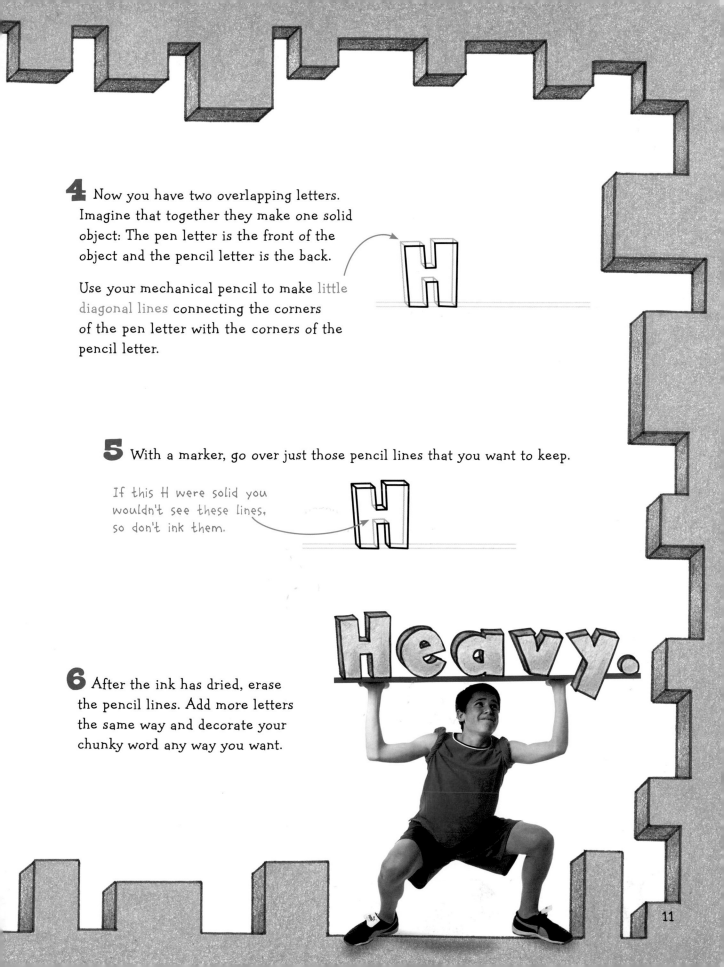

Shadow Letters

To add shadows to your letters, start the same way you did for chunky letters.

1 Outline a letter in pen and put another letter in pencil just below and off to one side.

2 Imagine that the pen letter is a solid wall and the pencil letter is hiding behind it. Use a colored pencil to shade just the parts of the pencil letter that can be seen around the edges of the wall. (Look at the picture to see what we mean.)

3 Lightly rub the eraser over the entire letter to remove the mechanical pencil marks. The colored pencil may fade a bit, so you might want to color in the shadows again.

4 Keep making letters the same way. Decorate your shadowy word any way you want.

flash!

glow

For a softer light effect, add a fuzzy edge to the outside of each shadow. Color very lightly in a loop-de-loop motion to get the fuzzy look.

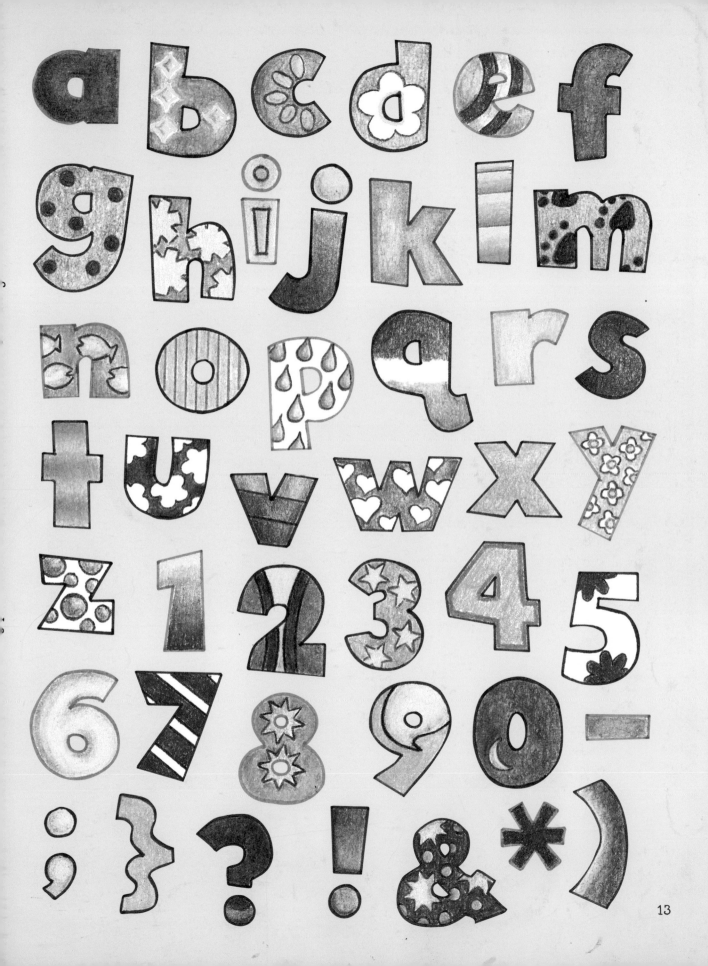

SPIFF UP
YOUR LETTERS

Use the tiny doodads on the green
stencil page to decorate any word.

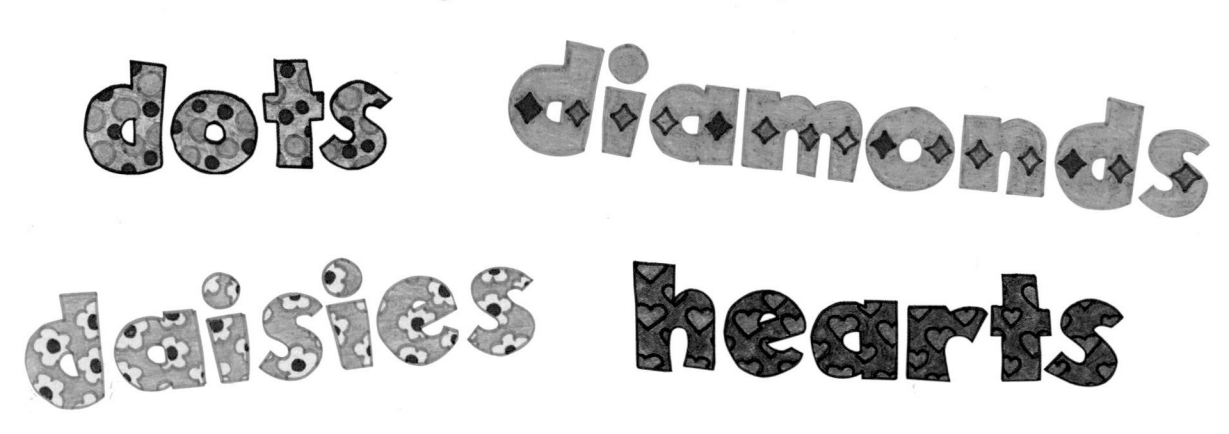

dots **diamonds** **daisies** **hearts**

Or try your own made-up designs.

plaid **Big City** **TULIPS** **FLAMES!** **beach** **vines**

Happy Birthday

THANKS LOVE

Illuminated

Letters

Decorating and framing any letter transforms it into a **Very Important Letter**, the kind that looks great at the start of a fairy tale or on a fancy certificate. Here's how to give your letter the **V.I.L.** treatment.

1 Find a half-shape you like on the green stencil page and pencil that stencil.

2 Flop the stencil sheet over to make the other half of the shape. Now you have a complete, enclosed frame.

3 Center a letter stencil inside the frame. Pencil it in.

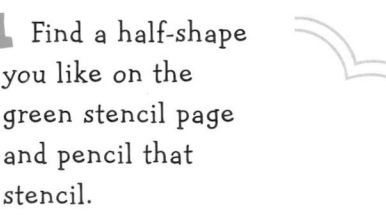

4 Decorate the letter and frame any way you like.

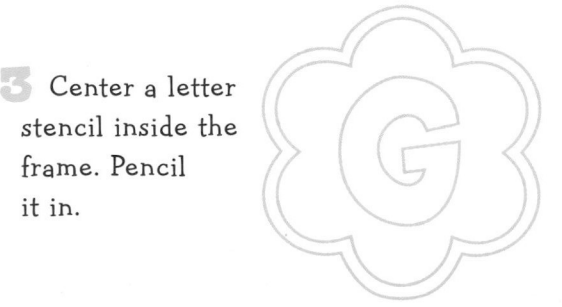

BRAND
YOUR BINDER

Protect your precious
vocabulary and math quizzes

by plastering your name on your binder.
That way you can't lose it even if you want to.

1 On the sticker paper, stencil separate illuminated letters that spell out your name. Decorate the letters and shapes any way you like.

2 Cut out each shape to make individual stickers.

Cut roughly around each shape first to separate it from the big sheet. Then cut carefully around the frame.

3 Peel off the adhesive backing and carefully stick each letter on your binder. **Classy!**

For a happy, no-homework-tonight feeling, let the stickers tilt and overlap each other.

~ BEYOND ~ BASIC ~ BASELINES

Messing with
the baseline adds
personality to your lettering.
Straight, horizontal lines are pretty plain vanilla.

For some real flavor, try

A WAVE

A SLANT

A CURVE

Remember to keep your baseline markings light so you can erase them later.

No vanilla here—
more like rocky road!

UP & DOWN

A B C D E F G

H I J K L M N

O P Q R S T

U V W X Y Z

? & ! @

Got Dots?

Adding decorative circles gives any skinny stencil letter a well-rounded personality.

1 Draw your baseline as usual – straight or curvy – and stencil a word on the line.

2 Pencil a circle stencil right on top of the first letter. Put the circle wherever it looks best (where two lines intersect, for example, or at the end of a line).

You'll find a tiny circle and a big circle on the green stencil. If you want an in-between-size circle, try the dot of the i on the orange stencil.

3 Keep stenciling circles on the letters until you finish the word.

4 Ink all the circles first. Then ink the letters.

Don't ink any letter lines that land inside a circle.

5 Carefully erase the pencil marks and decorate your letters any way you like.

Ain't dot cute?

Instead of circles, dot your letters with stencils of other tiny doodads.

flower   paw print

fish

butterfly   heart

Use the stenciled shapes as a starting point for designing your own doodads.

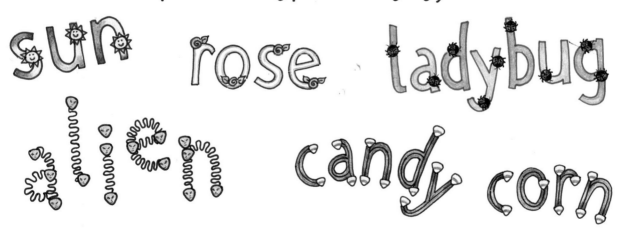

sun   rose   ladybug

alien   candy corn

Or skip the stencils and draw doodads from scratch!

strawberries

snowflakes

fortune cookies

swirls

flip-flops

yin-yang

candies

wheels

ice cream cones

kittens

skulls

holly

lucky horseshoes

shamrocks

notes

CURLICUE
Stencil Letters

Twist your words around with letter and swirl stencils.

1 Perch a letter stencil on your baseline and pencil it.

2 Use the swirl-shaped stencil to add curls on the ends of your letter. You don't have to curl every end. Just add a little flourish here and there.

3 Continue penciling letters and swirls until your word is done.

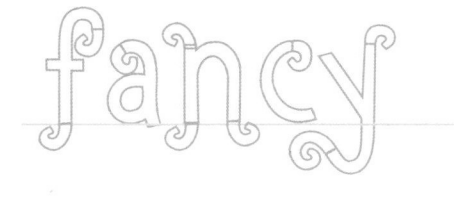

4 Outline the finished word in pen.

Don't ink swirls you don't want to keep.

5 When the ink is dry, erase the pencil. Decorate your letters any way you want.

Consider swirling just the first letter... or just the first and last letters... or go curly-crazy and swirl the whole word.

a b c d e f g h
i j k l m n o p
q r s t u v w
x y z 1 2 3 4)
5 6 7 8 9 0 }
* ; ; , , _

Letter a Door Sign
or two or three...

To make a sign strong enough to handle the ins and outs of your hectic life, reinforce it with thin cardboard. Cereal boxes work great for this.

1 Cut a panel from an empty cereal box.

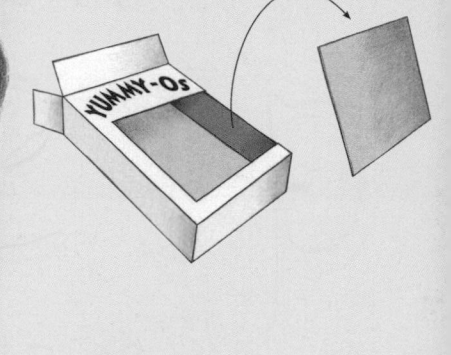

2 Use a glue stick or double-sided tape to cover the panel with construction paper.

3 Create your lettering on a sheet of plain paper and use a glue stick or double-sided tape to attach it to the construction paper.

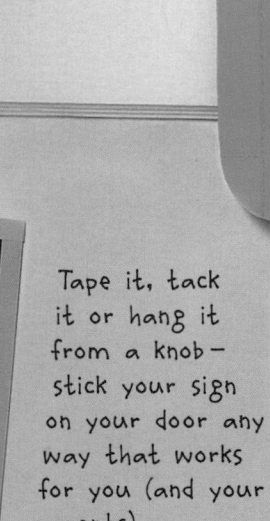

Tape it, tack it or hang it from a knob – stick your sign on your door any way that works for you (and your parents).

Who needs glue? Try cutting letters and shapes out of the sticker paper instead.

To make pockets for an IN/OUT sign, cut the bottom corners off an envelope and glue them to your sign.

For a fancy sign, use wrapping paper or foil in place of construction paper.

STENCIL-O-RAMA

There are at least a kajillion different ways you can use the stencils to make your own unique statement. Here are just a few.

CROWDED

overlapping solid letters

Slanty angles get letters in motion.

speedy!

gol╕ the stencil over for backward writing.

mirror

Lay the paper on top of the stencil to make a rubbing.

LOVE

Put an outline around your word, and then an outline around the outline, and then an outline around...

trippy

overlapping see-through letters

SQUSHY

Voila!

Try using a cute doodad stencil instead of the holes in the center of your letters...

LIGHTS

fab!

... or just skip the holes altogether.

to: Mom

Use the green stencil to make a tag that's any length you like.

ANTSY

Make stencil people

and pets!

POW!

For eye-popping perspective, pick a point and connect all your letters to it.

zoom

FREEHAND
lettering

Everything you can do with stencils, you can do freehand.

shadowy letters

wacky baselines

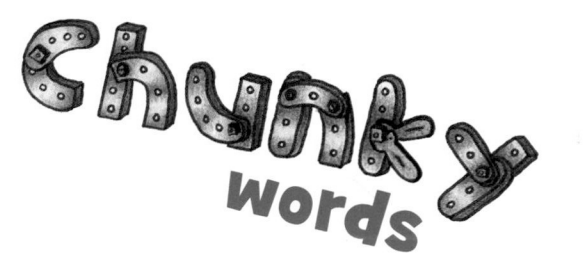
chunky words

dazzling designs

dinky DOODADS

Freehand letters may not look as perfect **as stencil letters but they can be a lot more** spontaneous **and** expressive. **All it takes is a little practice.**

On the following pages you'll find **TEN DIFFERENT ALPHABETS**. Each of them is stylish, unique and designed especially for you to use. Here's one way to try your hand at freehand lettering.

1 With the mechanical pencil, lightly write a word in simple letters.

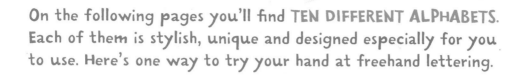

2 Copy the cool letters right on top of the simple ones. Think of a simple letter as a skeleton that holds a cool letter up.

Remember to keep your pencil marks very light.

3 Outline the finished letters in pen or colored pencil.

4 Carefully erase the mechanical pencil.

Of course, you can also **TRACE** the letters you like. It's a great way to get some practice making freehand letters.

5 Finish the word with any colors and decorations you want.

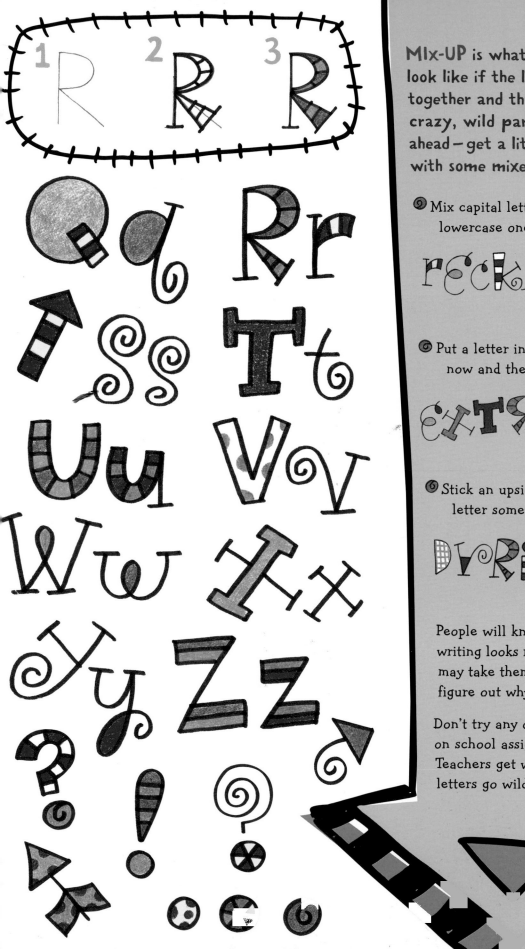

MIX-UP is what it would look like if the letters got together and threw one crazy, wild party. So go ahead—get a little wild with some mixed-up words.

- Mix capital letters with lowercase ones.

reckless

- Put a letter in backward now and then.

extreme

- Stick an upside-down letter somewhere.

during

People will know your writing looks radical, but it may take them a while to figure out why.

Don't try any of this craziness on school assignments. Teachers get worried when letters go wild.

31

JUST BEAD YOURSELF

To make a beautiful, sparkly nameplate, all it takes is double-stick tape and tiny seed beads.

1 On a piece of cardboard or heavy paper, spell out your name in double-stick tape.

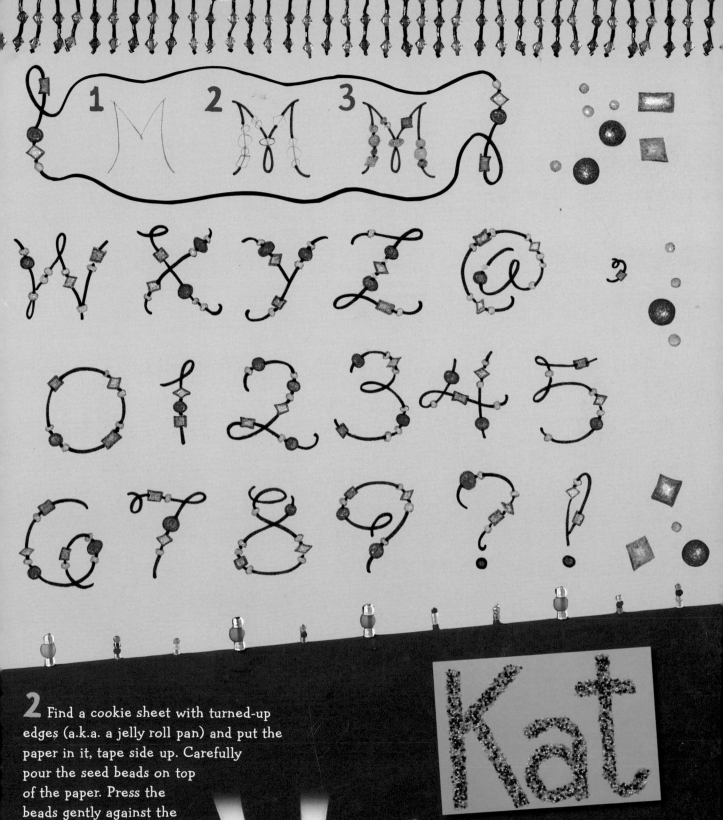

2 Find a cookie sheet with turned-up edges (a.k.a. a jelly roll pan) and put the paper in it, tape side up. Carefully pour the seed beads on top of the paper. Press the beads gently against the tape to make sure all the sticky parts are covered.

3 Lift the paper slowly out of the beads, letting the extra, unstuck ones fall back into the cookie sheet. Brilliant!

Swirlicue

A a B b C c
D d E e F f
G g H h I i J j
K k L l M m
N n O o P p

Here's an easy way to make two words look too cool.

1 Use a ruler to draw a neat rectangle. With the edge of the orange stencil, draw a wavy baseline right through the center of the rectangle.

2 Sketch out your letters for the first word. Try to fill up all the space above the wavy line, making the bottom edge of your word follow the line's curve exactly. The letters will look a little distorted, which is good.

SLUMBER

1 **S** **2** **S** **3** **S**

Qq Rr Ss Tt

Uu Vv Ww

Xx Yy Zz

! ' ~ @ ?

3 Sketch your letters for the second word. This time the top edge should follow the wavy line. Again, make your letters fill up the space entirely. Outline both words in pen.

You're Invited To A
SLUMBER PARTY

Carefully erase any stray pencil marks and then color your letters any way you like.

1 B 2 B 3 B

To make the bubbles **float** draw a shadow on the ground a little way below each letter.

Mm Nn
Oo Pp Qq !,
Rr Ss Tt @
Uu Vv
Ww Xx
Yy Zz

These letters also look great when you color them like balloons. Tie your word together in a balloon bouquet!

37

LETTER BETTER CARDS

It's a fact: People appreciate receiving the simplest hand-lettered card **WAY** more than the fanciest store-bought card. Ask anybody. Lettering a custom card is a guaranteed way to make any occasion a special occasion.

CONGRATS!

YOU'RE #1!

HAPPY FATHER'S DAY

You're a Star

Need a card QUICK?
Use the ready-made words on the green stencil. Simple!

Happy Birthday

THANKS LOVE

HELLO

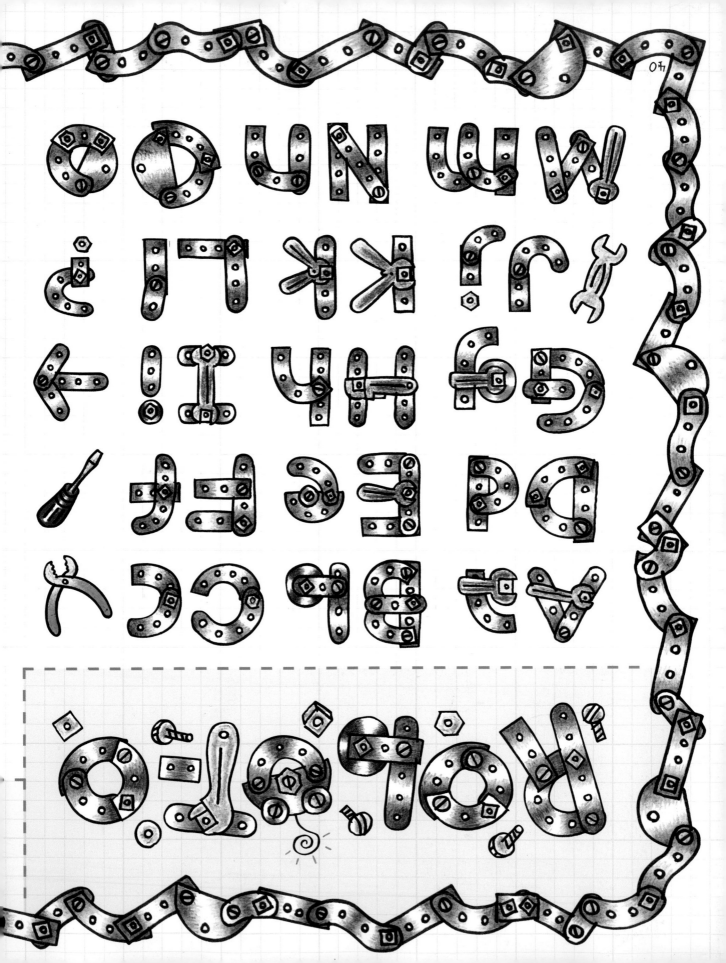

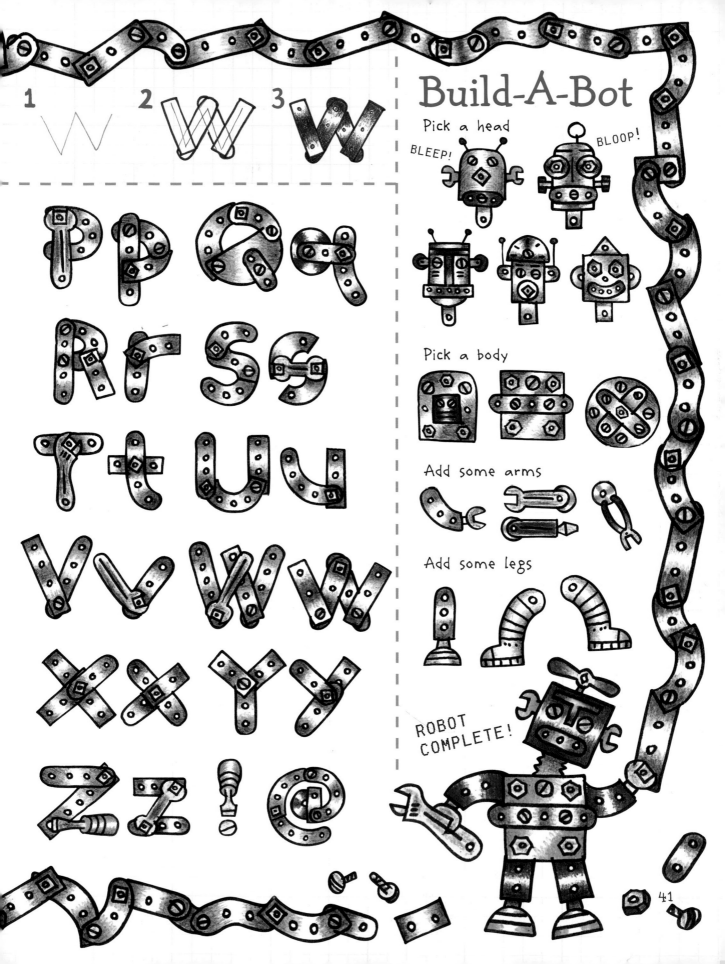

1 2 3

Build-A-Bot

Pick a head

BLEEP! BLOOP!

Pick a body

Add some arms

Add some legs

ROBOT COMPLETE!

41

Collect letters you love from everywhere:

magazines, newspapers, posters, old books, advertisements... anything with writing that rocks. Clip a sample out or, if you don't want to cut the original document, photocopy it. Keep your clippings in a special box or drawer and pull them out whenever you need lettering inspiration.

Simple lettering turns plain cookies (store-bought or homemade) into yummy birthday greetings.

2 Tbsp soft butter
2 cups confectioner's sugar
2 Tbsp milk
½ tsp almond or vanilla flavoring
food coloring

Beat together the butter, sugar, milk and flavoring until creamy. Divide up the frosting into a few little bowls and stir a drop of food coloring in each.

Spoon the frosting from one of the little bowls into one corner of a zippered plastic bag. Cut a tiny tip off the corner of the bag and squeeze the frosting onto your cookie.

StarBright

1   2   3

A   A   A

Aa Bb Cc Dd Ee

Ff Gg Hh Ii Jj

Kk Ll Mm Nn

Oo Pp Qq Rr Ss

Tt Uu Vv Ww

Xx Yy Zz

ALIEN ALPHABET

Use this handy code to keep your important communications out of the hands of prying Earthlings. Here's how it works:

Make the first stroke of a letter (in this case A) as you normally would.

/

Now write the rest of the letter to the left of your first stroke.

ᗷ/

Write single-stroke letters like C and J upside down.

Ɔ = C ∩ = J

That's it! Once you get used to it, Alien Alphabet is pretty easy to read and write – without using a decoder.

Depending on how you form letters, your Alien Alphabet might not look exactly like ours. That's fine. Just make sure that when the two parts swap places and join together, they form a normal Earth letter.

ᗷ/ = A		ᙏ١ = M
Ɛ١ = B		ᐯ١ = N
Ɔ = C		O = N...
Ɔ١ = D		ᴼ١ = P
Ɛ١ = E		ᴼ. = Q
=١ = F		ᖇ١ = R
⅂C = G		ᴢ = S
ⱶ١ = H		⌐١ = T
١١ = I		∧١ = U
∩ = J		ᐯ = V
⊲١ = K		ᙎ١ = W
⅂ = L		ᐱᐱ = X
		ᐱᐱ١ = Y
		⌐ = Z

47

1 (E

2 E

3 E)

OVERTIME
Try tackling these all-star alternates for Y and W.

0 1 2 3 4
5 6 7 8 9

D- !

QUALIFYING ROUNDS

If you don't like the letter O included in this alphabet, substitute one from your favorite sport. Consider a soccer ball, baseball, basketball, golf ball, bowling ball, hockey puck, tutu, Frisbee, pompom, volleyball, tennis ball, beach ball, Ping-Pong ball, kick ball, billiard ball, inner tube, hula hoop, softball, sumo wrestler... anything sporty and circular will do.

bloom

Aa Bb Cc Dd
Ee Ff Gg Hh
Ii Jj Kk Ll

twigs

Next time you're in the great outdoors, keep your eyes open for twig letters. Since anybody can bend, snap and tweak twigs into letters, finding twigs that are naturally letter shaped gives you extra points.

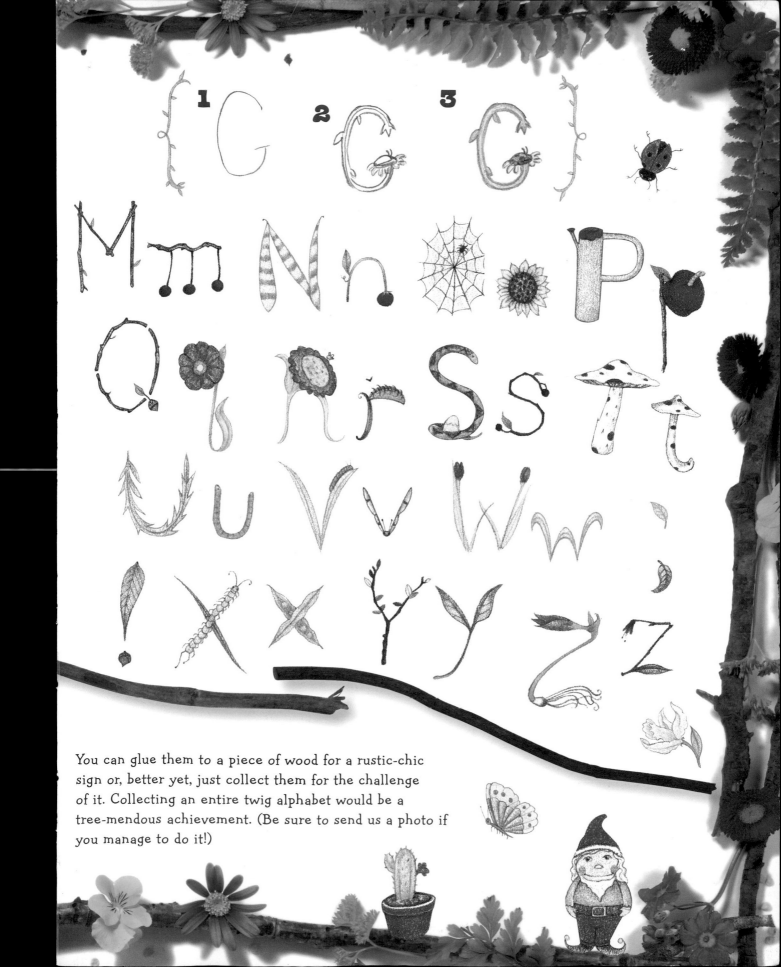

You can glue them to a piece of wood for a rustic-chic sign or, better yet, just collect them for the challenge of it. Collecting an entire twig alphabet would be a tree-mendous achievement. (Be sure to send us a photo if you manage to do it!)

Word Pictures

Making letters out of pictures like T H 1 S is like fitting lots of little ideas into one word.

For a really powerful statement, make your word look like one big idea. It's a great way to give any word a whole  WORLD of meaning.

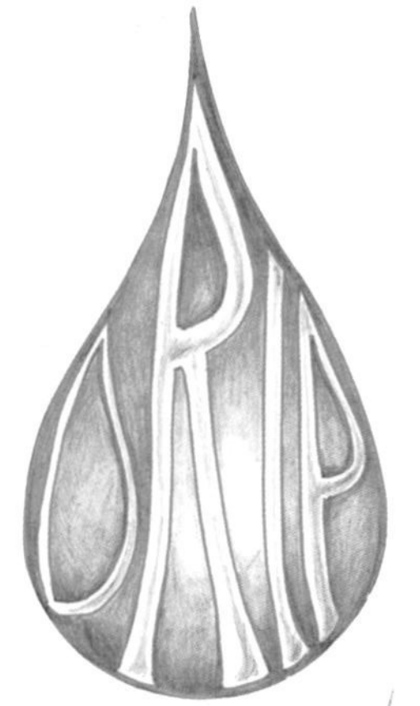

If you don't want to make the entire word into a picture, try just one letter.

ALOHA

lemon

float

ballet

Snake

Put a word picture on your next report cover and you'll get an A! *

*Maybe. No guarantees, of course. A lot depends on what you write in the report.

CREDITS

EDITOR
Karen Phillips

DESIGNER
Judy Wiatrek Trum

ART DIRECTOR
Kate Paddock

LETTER PERFECT
Patty Morris

CHICKEN SCRATCH
John Cassidy

PROJECT & LETTERING SAMPLES
Betsy Mitten, Eleanor Hanson, Teresa Roberts, Philip Wiatrek, Jammarie Mazzurco, Laurie Campbell, Paula Hannigan

INSTRUCTIONAL ART
Sara Boore

PHOTOGRAPHERS
Peter Fox, Joseph Quever

MODELS
Natalie Brock, Lainie Caswell, Mikaela Cooper, Keani Dame, EJ Floreal, Marina Foley, Jenner Fox, Radhika Khatod, Anthony Lim, Stephen Lim, Timmy Richardson, Soha Said, Rebecca Siegel, Marco Valente, Ying Vallone, Jordan Zenger and DeeDee the Dog

Alphabets

AM LH

A-BEAD-C
Nancy Hopkins

BR JC YJ
BUBBLY
Lizzy Rockwell

NM AS NK
ROBOT-O
Bud Peen

AM MTMG
STARBRIGHT
Leigh Wells

JC SL NS
SWIRLICUE
Julianna Smith

YN VT
BLOOM
Jaime Zollars

HL AP
MIX UP LH
Mary Anne Lloyd

AO DM
SCORE! LS
John Kerschbaum

CI JA
SURPRISE!
Jim Paillot

SL SR
VINTAGE
Sarajo Frieden

Show Us Your Genius!

Send us a photo of your craziest, coolest, quirkiest lettering and it may get displayed on the Fridge of Fame at klutz.com. That's world-wide recognition! To learn more, visit klutz.com or e-mail us at thefridge@klutz.com.

Can't get enough?
Here are two simple ways to keep the Klutz coming.

1 Get your hands on a copy of The Klutz Catalog. To request a free copy of our mail order catalog, go to klutz.com/catalog.

2 Become a Klutz Insider and get e-mail about new releases, special offers, contests, games, goofiness and who-knows-what-all. If you're a grown-up who wants to receive e-mail from Klutz, head to klutz.com/certified.

If any of this sounds good to you, but you don't feel like going online right now, just give us a call at 1-800-737-4123. We'd love to hear from you.

KLUTZ.com OPEN 24 HOURS
Come on in!

More Great Books from Klutz

Spiral Draw

Velvet Art

Crochet

Friendship Bracelets

Picture Tags™

Capsters™: Make Bottle Caps into Great Works of Coolness

Decorate Your Locker

Paper Stained Glass

It's All About Me: Personality Quizzes for You & Your Friends

Paper Fashions

Ribbon Purses

Picture Bracelets

Draw Thumb Animals

Doodle Dogs